MUDRA

Mudra

Early Poems and Songs

CHÖGYAM TRUNGPA

SHAMBHALA
Boston & London
2001

Shambhala Publications, Inc.
Horticultural Hall
300 Massachusetts Avenue
Boston, Massachusetts 02115
www.shambhala.com

© 1972 Chögyam Trungpa

Printed in the United States of America

⊗This edition is printed on acid-free paper that meets the
American National Standards Institute Z39.48 Standard.
Distributed in the United States by Random House, Inc.,
and in Canada by Random House of Canada Ltd

Library of Congress Cataloging–in–Publication Data

Trungpa, Chögyam, 1939–
Mudra: early poems and songs/Chögyam Trungpa.
p. cm.
English and Tibetan.
Includes index.
                    (pbk.)
1. Buddhist poetry, American. 2. Tibetan poetry—Translations into English.
I. Title.

PS3570.R84 M84 2001
811'.54–dc21

ISBN 978-0-87773-051-4

2001020588

To my guru Jamgön Kontrul Rinpoche

Homage to the Guru of Inner Awareness

The Body of the Dharma is in itself Peace,
And therefore it has never emerged from itself;
And yet Light is kindled in the womb,
And from the womb and within the womb the play of
  blessings arise;
That is to say, the energy of compassion begins its ceaseless
  operation.

One who follows the Buddha, Dharma and Sangha is aware
of Emptiness; that knowledge of Emptiness and of loving-
kindness which is without self is called the Great Perfection
of Equanimity, by means of which one has sight of this very
world as the Mandala of all the Buddhas.

May this guide you and be your companion in your
pilgrimage to Liberation; led by the Light of Wisdom, may
you attain to the form of the Great Compassionate One.

CONTENTS

Acknowledgements

The publishers wish to express their sincere thanks to the following for permission to quote from various works: Herbert V. Guenther, *The Life and Teaching of Naropa* (Oxford University Press); Charles Tuttle & Co., *Zen Flesh, Zen Bones*, by Paul Reps (for use of the Oxherding illustrations by Tomikichiro Tokuriki).

ཚེ་ཁ་ཀི་ཆི་རྒྱལ་ཆེན་བའ་ཚ་ཏན་ཏི་ད་གུ་གལ་ཡི་ཁ་ཡག་ཡི་ཚ་ཚལ། �

ཡ་ཚན་པ་ཏི་ཁུང་ བཚ་ཀི་ཏ་རྒུ་ཤི་ཀྲུ་ལ་ཡི་ཡི་ལ་རྫེ་ཡི་གཅང་ �

ཨ་ཀུ་རྒི་ཆ་ཀི་ལ་རི་ར་མི་ ཆི་ཡ་ར་སྐྱ་ལ་ཡ་ཕུ་ཡལ་ལ། �

ཤི་ཡོང་ སྒྲ་ལ་ར་ཀོ་ཡ་ར་ཚ་ཀི་རྒི་རྗི་ཡ་ལ་ཀ་ཡ་ལ་དྲི་ལ་ར་རྒུ། �

ག་ཛི་ཁ་ལ་ཡ་ཡིང་ ཚ་ཡ་རྒུ་ལྡ་རྒི་ར་ཡ་ར་ཚ་ཀ་ལ་ར་ཏི་རུ། �

རྒྱི་རྒི་ར་ཀི་ཚི་ལ་ལ་ སོ་ཡ་ཡ་ར་ཀི་ཡ་ར་ལ་ལ་ཀི་ར་ལ་ར་ཡི་ས་ན། �

ཆི་ར་རྒུ་ལ་ཨི་ཚི་ཀ་ལའི་ལི་ཀ་ལ་ར་ཚ་ཡ་ལ་ལི་ཡ་རྒུ་རྒི་ར་ར་ལ་ཡིགི། �

ར་ཆི་ཡ་ཕུ་ལ་ཡ་ཤི་ཡ་ཤ་ར་ འ་ར་ཡི་ར་ལ་ཚ་འ་རྒྱ་ར་ཕྱ་ར། ཀ་ཡ་ཀི་ར་ལ། �

ཚ་ར་རྗི་ལ་ཚི་ཡ་ད་ཡ་ར་ཡ་ནི། །

INTRODUCTION

It is a great pleasure that I can share some of my experiences with the world. The situation presents itself with publishing a small book called *Mudra* which is a selection of some of my songs and other spontaneous poems which I wrote since 1959 in Tibetan and English. I feel particularly blessed that I was able to include some works of authentic teachers: Jigme Lingpa and Petrül Rinpoche, which I have translated into English. As the crown jewel, this book carries these translations at its beginning. They are the vajra statement which frees the people of the dark ages from the three lords of materialism and their warfare.

It is the great blessing of the victorious lineage which has saved me from the modern parrot flock who parley such precious jewels like Mahamudra, Maha Ati and Madhyamika teachings on the busy market-place.

May I continuously gain health throughout my lives from the elixir of life which is the blessing of this lineage.

May I fearlessly beat the drum of the Dharma to wake sentient beings who fall asleep from desire, hatred and ignorance and deliver them to awakened state.

CHÖGYAM THE KUSULU

Maha Ati

THE TWO TRANSLATIONS that follow are from the work of two famed and much loved Tibetan teachers.

Petrül Rinpoche who wrote the poem addressed to Abushri lived at the end of the nineteenth century. He was a renowned Nyingmapa teacher, particularly interested in bringing the philosophy and practice of meditation together. He refused to live in an institutionalised monastery and became a great traveller.

Jigmê Lingpa lived at the time of the Fifth Dalai Lama. He was responsible for inspiring many people to study Maha Ati, which is the final and ultimate teaching of Buddha.

This teaching brings precise experiences of the awakened state. In fact, it surpasses concepts including the "idea" of Buddha nature, which has an element of the not yet mature. The difference between them seems to be that the achievement of Buddha nature is seen as a development, but with Maha Ati it is an experience all at once. The image of Maha Ati is the Garuda which emerges from the egg fully grown.

I have included these translations in the book even though they are advanced teaching because reading them seems to have inspired many people. There is no danger in presenting them because they are what is called *self-secret*, that is, one cannot understand what one is not ready for. Also they are incomplete without the transmission from a guru of the Lineage.

You who enjoy the union of bliss and emptiness
Seated motionless on the lunar disc
Above a beautiful hundred-petalled flower
Radiant with white light,
I pay homage to you the Divine Guru, Vajrasattva.

Listen, Abushri,
You miserable, daydreaming fool,
You remember how delusions
Confused you in the past?

15

Watch out for delusions in the present,
And don't lead a hypocritical life.

Stop unnecessary speculations.
You've made hundreds of plans
Which never came off
And only led to disappointment.
Unfinished acts are like
The overlapping action of the waves.
Stay alone and stop
Making your own head spin.

You've studied hundreds of philosophies
Without grasping any of them.
What's the point of further study?
You've studied without remembering
Anything when you needed it.
What's the point of contemplation?
Forget about your "meditation"!
It doesn't seem to be
The Cure for conflicting emotions.

You may have recited the set number of mantras
But you still haven't mastered the concrete visualisations.
You may have mastered the concrete visualisations
But you still haven't loosened the grip of duality.
You may have subdued apparent evils
But you still haven't tamed your ego.

Forget your set periods of meditation
And following an obsessive schedule.
High and clear but not letting go,
Low and steady but lacking clarity,
Penetrating insight but only stabbing—
That's your meditation!

Forget the stare of concentration
And the tethered mind.

Lectures sound interesting
But they don't help your mind.
The logical mind seems sharp
But it's really the seed of confusion.
Oral instruction sounds very profound
But it doesn't help if it isn't practised.
Forget about browsing through books
Which causes distraction and eyestrain.

You bang your antique prayer-drum,
But, just for the novelty of playing (with) it.
You offer up your body,
But in fact you're still attached to it.
You play clear-sounding cymbals
But your mind is heavy and dull.
Forget about these tricks,
Attractive though they are.

Your disciples seem to be studying
But they never follow through;
One day there's a glimmer of understanding,
But the next day it has gone.
They learn one thing out of a hundred
But they don't retain even that.
Forget these apparently fervent disciples!

One's closest friend is full of love
Today and indifferent tomorrow.
He is humble one minute and proud the next.
The more one loves him the more distant he becomes.
Forget the dear friend who smiles
Because the friendship is still a novelty!

17

Your girlfriend puts on a smiling face
But who knows what she really feels?
For one night of pleasure it's nine months of heartache.
You can spend a month trying to bed her and still not succeed.
It's really not worth all the scandal and gossip,
So forget about her.

Never-ending chatter stirs up likes and dislikes.
It may be amusing, and enjoyable
But it's merely imitating the faults of others.
The listeners seem receptive
But they may be critical at heart.
It only gives you a dry throat
So forget about idle talk!

Preaching without first-hand experience
Of the subject is like dancing on books.
The audience may seem willing to listen
But they're not really interested at all.
If you do not practise what you preach
You'll be ashamed of it sooner or later,
So forget about hollow rhetoric!

When you haven't any books
You feel the need for them;
When you have them you don't.
It's only a few pages
But to copy them is endless.
All the books in the world
Would give you no satisfaction,
So forget about copying—
Unless you get a fee for it!

One day you're relaxed,
The next you are tense.

You will never be happy
If you're swayed by people's moods.
Sometimes they are pleasant
But maybe not when you need them
And you might be disappointed.
So forget about politeness and flattery!

Political and religious activities
Are only for gentlemen.
That's not for you, my dear boy.
Remember the example of an old cow:
She's content to sleep in a barn.
You have to eat, sleep and shit—
That's unavoidable—anything
Beyond that is none of your business.
Do what you have to do
And keep yourself to yourself.

You're as low as the lowest
So you ought to be humble.
There's a whole hierarchy above you
So stop being proud.
You shouldn't have too many close associates
Because differences would surely arise.
Since you're not involved
In religious and political activities
Don't make demands on yourself.
Give up everything, that's the point!

This Teaching is given by **Yogi Trimê Lodrö** from his own
experience to his dear friend Abushri. Do practise it, although
there is nothing to practise. Give up everything—that's the
whole point. Don't get angry with yourself even if you can't
practise the Dharma.

NYING TIG
or THE INNERMOST ESSENCE

by Jigmê Lingpa

THIS is the Lion's Roar which subdues the rampant confusions
and misunderstandings of those meditators who have abandoned materialistic attachments to meditate on the Innermost
Essence.

The Maha Ati, which is beyond conceptions and transcends
both grasping and letting go, is the essence of transcendental
insight. This is the unchanging state of non-meditation in
which there is awareness but no clinging. Understanding this,
I pay ceaseless homage to the Maha Ati with great simplicity.

Here is the essence of the Maha Ati Tantra,
The innermost heart of Padmakara's Teachings,
The life-force of the Dakinis.
This is the Ultimate Teaching of all the Nine Vehicles.[1]
It can be transmitted only by a Guru of the Thought
　　Lineage
And not by words alone.
Nevertheless I have written this
For the Benefit of great meditators
Who are dedicated to the Highest Teaching.
This teaching was taken from the treasury of Dharmadhatu[2]
And is not created out of attachment
To theories and philosophical abstractions.

First the pupil must find an accomplished Guru with whom
he has a good karmic link. The Teacher must be a holder of
the Thought Lineage Transmission. The pupil must have

---

[1] The Nine Vehicles are: Shravakayana, Pratyekabuddhayana, Mahayana,
Kriyayana, Upayana, Yogayana, Mahayogayana, Anuyana and Atiyana.
[2] The Dharmadhatu is all-encompassing space.

single-minded devotion and faith, which makes possible the transmission of the Teacher's understanding.

The Maha Ati is of the greatest simplicity. It is what *is*. It cannot be shown by analogy; nothing can obstruct it. It is without limitation and transcends all extremes. It is clear-cut nowness, which can never change its shape or colour. When you become one with this state the desire to meditate itself dissolves; you are freed from the chain of meditation and philosophy, and conviction is born within you. The thinker has deserted. There is no longer any benefit to be gained from "good" thoughts and no harm is to be suffered from "bad" thoughts. Neutral thoughts can no longer deceive. You become one with transcendental insight and boundless space. Then you will find signs of progress on the Path. There is no longer any question of rampant confusions and misunderstandings.

Although this teaching is the King of the Yanas, meditators are divided into those who are highly receptive to it, those who are less receptive and those who are quite unreceptive. The most highly receptive pupils are hard to find, and it sometimes happens that Teacher and pupil are unable to find a true meeting point. In such a case nothing is gained and misconceptions may arise concerning the nature of Maha Ati.

Those who are less receptive begin by studying the theory and gradually develop the feeling and true understanding. Nowadays many people regard the theory as being the meditation. Their meditation may be clear and devoid of thoughts and it may be relaxing and enjoyable, but this is merely the temporary experiencing of bliss. They think this is meditation and that no one knows any better than them. They think "I have attained this understanding" and they are proud of themselves. Then, if there is no competent Teacher, their experience is only theoretical. As it is said in the Scriptures of Maha Ati: "Theory is like a patch on a coat—one day it will come apart". People often try to discriminate between "good" thoughts and "bad" thoughts, like trying to separate milk from water. It is easy enough to accept the negative experiences in life but much harder to see the positive experiences as part of the Path. Even those who claim to have reached the highest stage of Realisation are completely involved with worldly concerns and fame. They are attracted by Devaputra.[1] This means they have not realised the self-liberation of the six senses. Such people regard fame as extraordinary and miraculous. This is like claiming that a raven is white. But those who are completely dedicated to the practice of Dharma without being concerned about worldly fame and glory should not become too self-satisfied on account of their higher developments of meditation. They must practise the Guru Yoga throughout the four periods of the day in order to receive the blessings of the Guru and to merge their minds with his and open the eye of insight. Once this experience is attained it should not be disregarded. The Yogi should thenceforth dedicate himself to this practice with unremitting perseverance. Subsequently his experience of the Void will become more peaceful, or he will experience greater clarity and insight. Or again, he may begin to realise the shortcomings of discursive thoughts and thereby develop discriminating wisdom. Some individuals will be able to use both thoughts and the absence of thoughts as meditation, but it should be borne in mind that that which notes what is happening is the tight grip of Ego.

Look out for the subtle hindrance of trying to analyse experiences. This is a great danger. It is too early to label all thoughts as Dharmakaya. The remedy is the wisdom of nowness, changeless and unfailing. Once freed from the bondage of philosophical speculation, the meditator develops penetrating awareness in his practice. If he analyses his meditation and post-meditation experiences he will be led

[1] Devaputra personifies the evil force which causes attraction to sense objects.

astray and make many mistakes. If he fails to understand his
shortcomings he will never gain the free-flowing insight of
nowness, beyond all concepts. He will have only a conceptual
and nihilistic view of the Void, which is characteristic of the
lesser Yanas.

It is also a mistake to regard the Void as a mirage as
though it were merely a combination of vivid perceptions and
nothingness. This is the experience of the lower Tantras,
which might be induced by practise of the Svabhava Mantra.
It is likewise a mistake, when discursive thoughts are pacified,
to overlook the clarity and regard the mind as merely blank.
The experience of true insight is the simultaneous awareness
of both stillness and active thoughts. According to the Maha
Ati teaching, meditation consists of seeing whatever arises
in the mind and simply remaining in the state of nowness.
Continuing in this state after meditation is known as "the
post-meditation experience".

It is a mistake to try to *concentrate* on emptiness and, after
meditation, intellectually to regard everything as a mirage.
Primordial insight is the state which is not influenced by the
undergrowth of thoughts. It is a mistake to be on guard
against the wandering mind or to try and imprison the mind
in the ascetic practice of suppressing thoughts.

Some people may misunderstand the term *nowness* and take
it to refer to whatever thoughts happen to be in their mind
at the moment. *Nowness* should be understood as being the
primeval insight already described.

The state of non-meditation is born in the heart when
one no longer discriminates between meditation and non-
meditation and one is no longer tempted to change or
prolong the state of meditation. There is all-pervading joy,
free from all doubts. This is different from the enjoyment of
sensual pleasures or from mere happiness.

When we speak of "clarity" we are referring to that state
which is free from sloth and dullness. This clarity, inseparable

from pure energy, shines forth unobstructed. It is a mistake to equate clarity with awareness of thoughts and the colours and shapes of external phenomena.

When thoughts are absent the meditator is completely immersed in the space of non-thought. The "absence of thoughts" does not mean unconsciousness or sleep or withdrawal from the senses, but simply being unmoved by conflict. The three signs of meditation—clarity, joy and absence of thoughts—may occur naturally when a person meditates, but if an effort is made to create them the meditator still remains in the circle of Samsara.

There are four mistaken views of the Void. It is a mistake to imagine that the Void is merely empty without seeing the wild space of nowness. It is a mistake to seek the Buddha-nature (Dharmakaya) in external sources without realising that nowness knows no path or goal. It is a mistake to try to introduce some remedy for thoughts without realising that thoughts are by nature void and that one can free oneself like a snake unwinding. It is also a mistake to hold a nihilistic view that there is nothing but the Void, no cause and effect of karma and no meditator nor meditation, failing to experience the Void which is beyond conceptions. Those who have had glimpses of realisation must know these dangers and study them thoroughly. It is easy to theorise and talk eloquently about the Void, but the meditator may still be unable to deal with certain situations. In a Maha Ati text it is said:

"Temporary realisation is like a mist which will surely disappear."

Meditators who have not studied these dangers will never derive any benefit from being in strict retreat or forcibly restraining the mind, nor from visualising, reciting mantras or practising Hathayoga. As is said in the Phagpa Dūdpa Sutra,

"A Bodhisattva who does not know the real meaning of solitude,

Mudra

Even if he meditates for many years in a remote valley full
    of poisonous snakes
Five hundred miles from the nearest habitation,
Would develop overweening pride."

If the meditator is able to use whatever occurs in his life
as the Path, his body becomes a retreat hut. He does not
need to add up the number of years he has been meditating
and does not panic when "shocking" thoughts arise. His
awareness remains unbroken like that of an old man watching
a child at play. As is said in a Maha Ati text:

"Complete realisation is like unchanging space."

The Yogi of Maha Ati may look like an ordinary person
but his awareness is completely absorbed in nowness. He has
no need of books because he sees apparent phenomena and the
whole of existence as the Mandala of the Guru. For him
there is no speculation about the stages on the Path. His
actions are spontaneous and therefore benefit all sentient
beings. When he leaves the physical body his consciousness
becomes one with the Dharmakaya, just as the air in a vase
merges with the surrounding space when the vase is broken.

Songs

The Song of Separation

The one who makes known the Buddha not imagined by the
    mind,
The one who possesses the hidden teaching not shewn forth
    in books,
The one whose form is all wisdom, a true holder of the vajra,
Gangshar-wangpo, whose kindness can never be repaid,
I can take refuge in no one but you.
Yet you remain always within me:
You are my refuge, then, until Enlightenment.

Act according to the Dharma, and transgress it;
Keep to the straight path, and fall into sin.
Since I never found anyone I could rely upon,
Sever me from the barbarous and the degenerate.

In the kingdom of no two things,
Who are the rulers and the servants?
And since that is the land I'm travelling to,
Sever me from servants and attendants.

The senses weave their nets to entrap
Those riches that are theirs already;
Since unattachment is the path I follow
Sever me from the treasurer of attachment.

The ownerless estate of meditation
Is built according to a perfect equanimity;
Since love and hate shall find no place therein,
Sever me from the monastery of possessiveness.

The yogin who lives only in the hour
Is the favoured one of all kingdoms;
And since there is no need to reckon gifts and honour,
Sever me from the appearance of devotees.

Knowledge of being is the perfect teacher
And he is with me everywhere I go;
Since he it is I am relying on,
Sever me from those who speak for sect or party.

II

Ever present in the womb of joy
Remains the Mandala of the Five Wisdoms;
And since that is the only thing that's real,
Sever me from the gods of mankind's making.

Samsara and Nirvana do not stand opposed:
There's one that rituals will never reach;
Since I can overcome the mind's duplicity,
Sever me from the mind-made guardian deities.

The fatherland is with you everywhere,
Awareness will maintain its own defence;
Since there's no need to build up your self-centredness,
Sever me from Samsara's local gods.

Armed with the sword of faith in contemplation,
One stroke will free one's powers to realise all things;
Since this is the weapon that my teacher gave me,
Sever me from the hatred roused by patriotic war.

Nothing is dependable, nothing is fruitful;
The sun shines cheerfully, and yet
The darkness thickens and a reddening sky surrounds us.
What is there left that I can do?

I want to leave everything behind me,
Even if I'm ignorant of the Dharma.

Even if you're ignorant of the Dharma,
Chögyam, just you surrender everything.

My guide the hidden, joyful light of the teaching,
May the blank darkness round about me disappear.
Living the life of a young wandering mendicant,
May I guide the world to a world beyond itself.

The Valley of Mystery, Tibet, 1959

Song of the Golden Elephant

The eagle soars away into the sky
And yet he never plumbs the depths of space.
The four seasons give place to one another,
Yet never seem to have an end or a beginning.
When the one dry tree on the hill is blown down
By the timely wind, what can one do?

The whistling winter wind blows lightly
The white flowers of the snow-flakes.
Remembering the mother herding yaks,
How can one ever forget the highland of Gejê?

O pillar of the sky, high mountain peak,
Hills, where trees and grasses grow, surround you,
Yet you remain alone and still,
The cloud of peace wrapped round about your shoulders.
Remembering the fatherland

31

The white flag is fluttered by the song of sadness.
The beautiful form of Jomo Lhari mountain
Comes suddenly to mind
And only the liquid turquoise of the lake
Can comfort me.

The East side and the West side of the hill are seen together
And the white banner that is thereupon
Speaks of that thing far off yet close at hand.

A young and golden elephant I offer you.
Beware the baby elephant
Still in the jungle,
The lonely child who drinks the hot fresh milk.
When he presents you with a crystal mirror
Make out the golden syllables
Written on my heart.

Read this by the light of the torch that dispels darkness.

Two cuckoos yesterday, by destiny
Were met together on a bush in South Tibet.
They sang so beautifully the huntsmen there
Forgot their arrows, poisoned with black hatred.

The learned men, interpreting,
Pull out all the commentaries
And eat their own flesh in secret.
Stupid and ignorant then, he weeps.
Do you not see him also
Shouting at stones?

The cranes went winging their way homeward
When the life of the thin one, the diseased one,
The life of the one with no strength in his wings

Was cut short by the sharp winter.
Do not blame god for this,
Calling him heartless.

Some fly in the sky and some sleep,
But none can cross time's circling street.
Horses gallop, have no destination.
An arrow also killed the cunning fox.

Fire engines guard the North, South, East and West
But when the house of god itself begins to burn
The scorching of his hair ascends to heaven
And none can halt the raging wind of karma.

The rain clouds gather in the clear blue sky,
And suddenly I saw their glaring face
Red eyed as a full moon in eclipse.

Who was it uttered these black incantations
And eighteen lightnings swarming, scorching hot
And all the valley a great wave of blood
And all the world's cry one tongue?

Cool off these fires, Avalokiteshvara.
Your smiling face is all compassion,
Your long, white, smooth, thin arm is stretched to save
And light glows in a peaceful ring around you.

Freed from the mind's habitual duplicity,
What need is there for wordless liberation?
Illumination breaks through everywhere,
The fires of suffering fade and disappear.
Come with me and wash off your leprosy,
Bathe in elixir from the crystal vase
And joining hands with me come on to liberation.

The Silent Song of Loneliness

The one to whom peace and solitude
Are known for ever, perfectly,
You, Milarepa, Longchenpa,
The Guru to whom all things are known,
The one who shows the single truth,
You I remember, I, your son.
Crying from an alien island.

The wild duck, companionless,
Cries out in desolate loneliness,
And flies alone, wings outspread,
Soaring in the boundless sky.

In the womb beyond the one and many
Yours is the inner loneliness,
And yours alone the emptiness
Within and everywhere around.
The mountainside alone creates
The clouds that change the rain, the two
That never go beyond the one,
So soar away, wild duck, alone.

Thunder resounding everywhere
Is only the elements at play,
The four expressing the sound of silence.
The hailstones triangular,
The black clouds and the storms blast,
Are earthbound only, wild duck,
So do not fall a prey to doubt
But get you gone upon your flight.

The waters of the sunset lie
Saffron-painted, beautiful,

And yet unchanging is the light
And dignity of the sun; so cut
The cord that joins the day and night,
And stretch your wings and fly, wild duck.

The moon's rays spread over the ocean
And heaven and earth smile: the cool
And gentle breeze moves over them,
But you are young and far from home,
Wild duck. So stretch your wings alone
And travel on the path to nowhere.

II

A sharpness is on the Summer's tail;
The healing breeze of Summer yields
To the bitter wind of Winter time.
If this was a signal to you, bird,
Then you would know the seasons not
Themselves, but as a turning wheel.

The young deer, wandering among
The Summer green and pleasant ways,
Remembering his mother caught
And killed in a trap, can yet enjoy
The freedom of the empty valley
And find relief and rest of mind.

The lonely child who travels through
The fearful waste and desolate fields,
And listens to their barren tune,
Greets as an unknown and best friend
The terror in him, and he sings
In darkness all the sweetest songs.

The lonely bird lived all his days
In a place apart, yet did not know
Peace, or the dwelling-place of peace.
But when the face of loneliness
Is known to you, then you will find
The Himalayan hermitage.

The jungle child sings his song
Sad and alone, yet weeps for nothing,
And joy is in him as he hears
The flute the peaceful wind is blowing.
And even so am I, in the sky
Dancing, riding the wild duck.

24 June 1965

Song of the Dakini

I

I praise the Queen of Means who goes gathering riches,
The Queen of Wisdom who subdues the three-fold world,
The dancer in the womb of all-pervading goodness,
I praise the one who overcomes and calms.

Peacemaker, who sends out the light of quietness,
Whose beaming smile lies behind the world,
Who gathers up the ocean of life's bounty
Into the womb of gladness, you I praise.

Creator of the light of dignity
And opener of the door of happiness,
The door of wisdom and of quality
And those four doors which open ever inwards,

Passionate, ruddy-faced, you calmly dance;
You are the great enchantress of true love.
O let me praise you as the dakini
Whose passions are unfettered, unperturbed.

Wrathful and cruel, with red eyes glaring
You shatter the rigid barriers of the dark.
O let me praise you, whose miraculous anger
Is for the sufferer the way to joy.

I honoured you, the only mother, yet
Uncertain and confused, I failed to set
You in your place in the eternal mantra.
Forgive me, grant me your transcendant power.

Your face is brighter than the sun and moon,
Your looks are of peaceful or of wrathful love,
But I was blinded by duality.
You are the Queen of Heaven; think on me.

II

The gestures of your hands showed me their meanings
And as you danced the bells rang at your belt;
I could not then truly interpret them—
Now, dakinis, come under my control.

Ever apparent, you do not exist,
Only a word utters you here with us.
Waistless, formless, goddess of the real,
Now we may make known the secret prophecy.

Unseen, you are the mother of the Buddhas;
Yet seen, creation's power is your deceit.
As an arc of light in the middle path, conduct
The envoys of the body's force to freedom.

The cruel devils and the harmless gods
And the grey folk that hustle in between
Make up the array of these impulses.
Command the onslaught and commence attack!

Keep the path clear of those too youthful
And, whether as human being or as goddess,
Devil or vampire, dance entrancingly;
For each of us disperse the darkness of this age.

Among the Buddhas you are a Vajra-yogini,
In the land of Karma you are the great hostess,
On earth you bear a hundred thousand names,
Formless, you yet sum up the universe.

As mother of us, or as daughter,
Take us to where we realise the truth.

In the sea of my mind the words as waves have risen
In recollection of the Great Queen.
May the Ocean benefit
Those who sail beyond the great sea.

Fall 1965

Poems

The Victoria Memorial

In the garden of lusts craving burgeons,
The darkness of sin lies thick on the crumbling field;
The flames of the age of darkness flare in the place of terror
And Chögyam only is left.

Drops of blood cover the bamboo leaf
And a terrible wind from the graveyard scatters the name of
  the dead.

The accents of the land echo even in heaven;
Now my world is only a name.

The wind howls in the dark wood
And the wheeling birds have nowhere to settle;
Whom can I tell, when the beautiful pine tree
Cracks with her cones and comes splintering down.

Death leers up from under the earth;
Remembering the love of the only beloved
I fall to the ground, and my cries fill every direction.

And O, the white child, and his mother with her bracelets of
  turquoise,
Appears in a moment, and "welcome, welcome" cries;
(Ask still the same question concerning the stain on the
  mirror.)

Here in this alien place the orphan stands naked,
Preparing to find and to found a new fatherland,
Licking the honey that flows from the glistening hives.

So fair, and yet not the moon,
So bright, and yet not the sun,

More perfectly set than the stars in the heaven,
I saw in her beauty the whole of the universe,
And you I took as a friend, with love.

If it is the moon in the sky—
quite enough to show your smiling gesture.
If it is the moon in your mind—
How then to show your smiling gesture?

I have no pride
in being a unicorn
if you consider this carefully
you might be able to
relax your struggle.

Even if he is the prince of a kingdom
trust him and ask him some questions.
Since he is a human being
You'll be able to get some answers.

If one recollects suffering
of arrow piercing into the heart
one should remember the beloved one
and compare the feelings.

If you have a sharp sword
learn to cut off the life of your enemy
If you have doubt in your mind
who's going to cut that uncertainty?

Whatever comes out of the mind,
regard not that as poetry.
When the true poetry comes,
no such question exists.

Yesterday I returned from the battlefield
Since then I'm able to rest
Please do not hope that today
I'll be able to defeat more enemies.

The moon rises, the sun has set
planets rotate in their orbit
Yet the heavens will not change
This we discover in each other.
Do not hope for too much—
results might bring painful disappointment
If you remain without any doubts
That is the wish-fulfilling gem.

I have no name
but others call me "the nameless one".

How can one escape imprisonment
and burst the chains of concept?

1969

In the wilds of the Deer Park in Sarnath
There are the monasteries and shrines, relics of Buddhism.
A stray dog finds a wounded deer lying in a shed
And licks it in an attempt to try and heal the wound,
But the interior damage is impossible to reach with this
    automatic act of the tongue.

Look! Look! There is a burning heart;
The flames like sunset or an eclipse of the sun,
The dark red of the end of an eclipse.
Some kind-hearted person runs to the nearest telephone
But there is no rescue, no doctor who can extinguish this
    fire without body,

Though it is courageous at least to try to hold on to the heart.
Yet it is deeply sad that he had to let it go this far.

What is compassion? What is love?
When the lover and the love become one in the simplicity of
    the present.
Still pain and pleasure lie in the midst of a bundle of steel
    wool
And light and dark live in the midst of lamentation.
Who helps—because the saviour and the victim both need
    help.

The dog patiently tries to heal the wound of the deer of
    Sarnath.
The burning sun dries up not only the trees, plants and
    streams, but a whole continent.

Who will make the rain?
Who will invoke the clouds?
Where is the formless form of Compassion,
The Compassion of Avalokiteshvara?

                                            March 12, 1969

Who is lost?
And who lost?
In any case, never discovered;
But there remains complete devotion.
It seemed not necessary to find where one should attach
    oneself as object of devotion.

In the highland where the wild animals patiently graze
On grass which is dry,
Merely waiting for the fresh greenness to grow.

Biting cold wind which is more than memory,
With a heartless, cutting snowstorm.
Wild geese sing in the distance,
Aimlessly, the fox and jackals run about.
A hardened traveller on horseback rides across the horizon.
Beautiful things, all these.
Yet impenetratingly desolate.
It is almost hard to see the inspiration to enjoy the scene.
But someone noticed these,
Even to the movement of tiny grasses blown by the cold wind.

Completely intoxicated by you,
This longing for Padma Trimê.
There is nothing to conceal,
Yet hardly anything to expose
For my faith and devotion is beyond word or melody of music.
A kind that no one would be able to hear or understand.

It is beautiful to grow with this loneliness,
Since it is your aloneness which inspires and drives me into
    selfless action.
The echo of your voice is heard.
The expression of your face is seen.
But when I become acquainted with these,
There is no more longing,
But the infinite compassion is inherited by your son.
You thrust upon me this weight.
I know it will remain as burden
Until I see your face in me,
And hear your voice from everywhere.

This is you Padma Trimê:
Ornamented with yogi costumes,
Dancing on a cloud,
Singing in the language of Dakinis—

You are the fire and water,
You act as the earth and the space
Which accommodate the infinite.

March 28, 1969

So much for love.
In the state of meditation and openness
There comes dukha;
Suffering is the nature of
Samsara.

The old traveller,
Stumbling with his stick's support
Makes the journey of pilgrimage.
Each step is not perfect.
Walking on the desert sand,
His foot slips as he walks.
Slow and long
On the arduous journey
He hears the sound of the
Grains of sand
Yet firmly plants his steps
In the sand
As his support.

Of course, I know—
Of course, it is shown to me—
Of course, there's no doubt—
The play of Dakinis
Is always there.

In love
I feel both pain and pleasure
Which is quite clearly seen
In the nature of Dakinis.

Sometimes it is tedious,
Tedious because you're hopeful,
Hopeful for something to happen.
Sometimes it is creative
And your heart is open
To creativity.
These two manifestations
Are clearly seen
Alternatively,
Pain and pleasure alike.
It is what is.
That is what I have found.
In pain there's no sickness
Because pain is aroused
By creative forces.
Thanks to Dakinis.
The same goes for pleasure,
The same goes for love.
Love is something profound
Something deeper—
In fact it's the flow
Of the universe.
Without love nothing is created.

I'm lying in bed as a patient.
Beside me is the quadrapod
Which helps me to walk.
There are so many friends
Who are longing to give
Their own health for my recovery.
Still it is the play of love.
Here I see that love
Consists of both pleasure and pain.
Love is the expression or gesture
Of apparent phenomena.

It is painful as though someone
Controlled the beat of my heart,
As though someone had stolen my heart.
But underneath lies inspiration.
So I discover
That she who has stolen my heart
Is the true Shakti
Who removes all possessiveness.
People can die for love
Quite involuntarily.
People have such courage in love.
Pain and pleasure are one in love.
For it includes negative thoughts,
Possessiveness,
Impermanence.
This love and the nature of love
Can never be changed
By anyone.
It is the dance of the Dakinis.
It is the dance of the Kagyü Lineage.
As historically Gampopa,
Living in a monastery,
The father of the Kagyü School,
Let loose his three precious
Chief disciples,
Let them dance and
Compose music
In the state of ecstasy.

I've said so much
In this poem.
But a poet's mind
Can never stop composing.
He identifies himself with the play of Dakinis
Or that of Sarasvati.

This poem is the discovery
Of love in courage and freedom
Glory be to the subject—
Poetry.

Newcastle General Hospital
Spring 1969

The Perfect Love Poem

There is a beautiful snow peaked mountain
With peaceful clouds wrapped round her shoulders.
The surrounding air is filled with love and peace.
What is going to be is what is,
That is love.

There is no fear of leaping into the immeasurable space of
    love.
Fall in love?
Or, are you in love?
Such questions cannot be answered,
Because in this peace of an all-pervading presence,
No one is in and no one is falling in.
No one is possessed by another.

I see a beautiful playground
Which some may call heaven,
Others may regard it as a trap of hell.
But, I, Chögyam, don't care.

In the playground beautiful Dakinis are holding hand drums,
    flutes and bells.
Some of them, who are dancing, hold naked flames, water, a
    nightingale,
Or the whole globe of earth with the galaxies around it.
These Dakinis may perform their dance of death or birth or
    sickness,
I am still completely intoxicated, in love.
And with this love, I watch them circle.
This performance is all pervading and universal,
So the sonorous sound of mantra is heard
As a beautiful song from the Dakinis.
Among them, there is one dakini with a single eye,
And turquoise hair blown gently by the wind.
She sends a song of love and the song goes like this:
    HUM HUM HUM
    If there is no joy of Mahamudra in the form,
    If there is no joy of Mahamudra in the speech
    If there is no joy of Mahamudra in the mind,
    How would you understand
    That we Dakinis are the mother, sister, maid and wife.
And she shouts with such penetrating voice, saying
    Come, come, come
    HUM HUM HUM
    Join the EH and VAM circle.

Then I knew I must surrender to the dance
And join the circle of Dakinis.
Like the confluence of two rivers,
EH the feminine and VAM the male,
Meeting in the circle of the Dance.

Unexpectedly, as I opened myself to love, I was accepted.
So there is no questioning, no hesitation,
I am completely immersed in the all-powerful, the joyous
    Dakini mandala.

And here I found unwavering conviction that love is universal.
Five chakras of one's body filled with love,
Love without question, love without possessions.

This loving is the pattern of Mahamudra, universal love.
So I dance with the eighty Siddhas and two thousand aspects
   of Dakinis,
And I will dance bearing the burden of the cross.
No one has forsaken me.
It is such a joyous love dance, my partner and I united.

So the clear, peaceful mountain air,
Gently blows the clouds,
A beautiful silk scarf wrapped round.
The Himalayas with their high snow peaks are dancing,
Joining my rhythm in the dance,
Joining with the stillness, the most dignified movement of
   them all.

August 6, 1969

Life   Was as it WAS

                                  moon

     me

   rock

   rock   grasssssssssssssssss windgrass

    rock

     but it's cold   cooooooooooooooooooooooool ling

and rockieeeeessssssssssssssssssssssss but waterrrrrrrrrrrr

Past and Present

If you are a king of an empty field
There is no need for a queen.
If you are a madman in desolate mountains
There is no need for a city.

When I met you yesterday
You wore red clothes
When I talked to you today,
You would be better unmasked.

I was born naked.
My beloved parents
Kindly gave me a name.
When I reached twenty
I thought "a name is a chain,
I want to abandon it".
Whoever I question
No one answers me.
When I hear the wind in the pines
I get an answer.

August 9, 1969

Early Outward

Get up today!
The sun is shining brightly.
Listen—you are the essence of my heart;
the goodness of life.
I invite you—Get up today.

Today's gone very quickly—
tomorrow will come.
Please do not give up your hope
that we will have time to taste
happiness and
sorrow.

If you are the moon in heaven
show me your face as full moon.
If this is the season of summer
show me the rhododendron flowers.

On the mirror of the mind
many reflections could have occurred.
However, the face of the beloved one
cannot be changed.

If the heart has any pattern,
there can be no change.
Will the sun rise tomorrow?
—It is useless to ask such silly questions.

Whether the sun arises or not,
I don't make any distinctions.
My care is only for you—
that in your heart the genuine sun should rise.

If she is my dearly beloved one
she should be called "One who has stolen my heart".
The dance of apparent phenomena—mirage.
Is this performed by you?

When I meditate in the cave
rock becomes transparent.
When I met the right consort
my thought became transparent:

Dearly beloved,
    to whom my Karma is linked,
    I could not find anyone but you.
    The wind of Karma is a force
    beyond my control.
This good aspiration and karma
is impossible to change.
Turbulence, waterfall of Kong Mê—
no one can prevent it.

When my mind recalls the dearly beloved
there is no shyness or fear;
majestic dakini as you are—
this must be my good karma.

                                    1969

I have no hope or expectation
yet a wish has been fulfilled,
just like snow-flakes in winter
form into eight-petalled flowers.

You are the Queen.
You produce
Famine, war, disease
And also happiness.
I salute you.

The Queen must be subdued
As she has been in the past.

I see you peering through the clouds
With your single eye.
You pretend to hide your name
But I know your name is
Ekājati.

Come, accept my feast offering.
Take part in the dance along with the other dakinis.
Whether you manifest yourself
As harmful demon
Or protectress
You have but one form all the time.

Why, why do you have to show such reaction?
I know because you are a red bitch
Who clings to one thing.

Do you remember the message of Padmasambhava?
At that very moment he put his vajra on your head,
He plunged you in the boiling lake
And showed your true form,
A naked skeleton.

I am the descendant of Padmakara
As you very well know.
Time has very little to do with it.

Don't please confuse in the wire wool,
Don't please confuse in this passionate flame.
Remember your vow.
In the end,
You and I become one,
Yet that is no threat for your existence.

Come, Come Ekajati.
Bow to me,
Bow to my wisdom.

November 2, 1969

You disguise in the darkness
You disguise in the brilliance of sunlight.
Your single eye appears

As the sun's eclipse.
You bring along with you
All your retinue;
The harmful demons
The seductive girl.
Some ride on reindeers
Holding their vajra sceptres
Heart and corpse.
Some ride on garudas.
Some ride on swans
Making a rain of flowers.

You carry sacks of poison
That could destroy the whole universe
You also carry the crystal container of medicine
Elixir that could cure
The sickness of all human beings.
You appear as harmful demon
And protectress.

I Chögyam am not afraid
Whatever form you take
For I have seen you in every possible form.

Take my offerings.
Obey my commands.
As Padmakara subdued you
On the pass of Mount Hêpo
In Samyê.

I am the descendant of Padmakara;
It is not your wish that counts.
It is time for you to submit
And fulfil the desires of my work
As you did in Samyê.

I know your origin,
Born out of an iron boil.
I know your mischievous actions.
I have your sacred heart mantra
And your words of promise
In the presence of Padmakara.
Be my sister
Or mother or maid.
Do not interrupt me any more
This is the command
Of Vidyadhara.

Understand Dakinis
As the universal force;
That is to understand
The true force within your mind.
It is unborn, unoriginated.
Understand this.

November 3, 1969

Looking into the world
I see alone a chrysanthemum,
Lonely loneliness,
And death approaches.
Abandoned by guru and friend,
I stand like the lonely juniper
Which grows among rocks,
Hardened and tough.
Loneliness is my habit—
I grew up in loneliness.
Like a rhinoceros
Loneliness is my companion—
I converse with myself.
Yet sometimes also,

Lonely moon,
Sad and Happy
Come together.

Do not trust.
If you trust you are in
Others' hands.
It is like the single yak
That defeats the wolves.
Herds panic and in trying to flee
Are attacked.
Remaining in solitude
You can never be defeated.
So do not trust,
For trust is surrendering oneself.
Never, never trust.

But be friendly.
By being friendly towards others
You increase your non-trusting.
The idea is to be independent,
Not involved,
Not glued, one might say, to others.
Thus one becomes ever more
Compassionate and friendly.
Whatever happens, stand on your own feet
And memorise this incantation:
Do not trust.

25 November 1969

Red glaring from the West
Sound of raindrops—
Such a peculiar climate
And a rainbow too.

60

Freedom,
Freedom from limitations,
Freedom from the square
(Exact patterns all carefully worked out),
Freedom from mathematical psychology
And logic.
The banner of true and free
Flies in the air of the middle way.
It is somehow wholesome,
Healthy as the energetic tiger
Or lion.
Growl,
GROWL—
Beautiful pointed teeth
Demonstrating invincibility.
I, Chögyam, watch all this
From the top of a pine tree
Bending in the wind
Quite nonchalantly.

                                    December 16, 1969

Three bladed missile
Piercing to the sky—
Vroom,
Bang, Bang!
It leaves the ground.
It is the manifestation of hatred
For the whole earth,
Hatred for this whole solar system.
Who is the victim?
Who is the victor?
It is highly ironical
While others live on
Such luxury.
There must be some force of

Truth and justice—
These very words have been over used.
Yet with the force of the true powerful nature
There will be the perfect situation
Which is unorganised,
Inspired by the pupil who is not conditioned.
So the world is not
All that pitch black—
There is some harmony
And in this harmony we live.
We have been inspired
Yet are neither anarchists
Nor revolutionaries
In the blind sense.
Love to you all.

December 17, 1969

The Way of the Buddha

Walking the hidden path of the Wish-fulfilling Gem
Leading to the realm of the heavenly tree, the changeless.
Untie the tongues of mutes.
Stop the stream of Samsara, of belief in an ego.
Recognise your very nature as a mother knows her child.

This is transcendent awareness cognisant of itself,
Beyond the path of speech, the object of no thought.
I, Tilopa, have nothing at which to point.
Knowing this as pointing in itself to itself.

Do not imagine, think, deliberate,
Meditate, act, but be at rest.
With an object do not be concerned.
Spirituality, self-existing, radiant,
In which there is no memory to upset you
Cannot be called a thing.

> By Tilopa. Translated by Herbert V. Guenther
> in *The Life and Teaching of Naropa*.

THE WAY OF THE BUDDHA

THE path of spiritual development in the Buddhist tradition is described in terms of yanas or vehicles. At each stage along the path, particular methods are employed to take the meditator or yogi to the next stage. In this chapter we briefly describe all nine stages of psychological development and the appropriate vehicles for travelling through them in the hope that some insight into the subtlety and depth, as well as the logic of the experiences involved, will inspire people to enter or persevere on the path. We hope this description will also serve as a caution for those who are overly ambitious or complacent. It should be clear to all who read it that a competent guide is needed since the tendency towards self-deception becomes increasingly dangerous as one progresses on the path.

All the Buddhist traditions in Tibet contain the Three-Fold Yanas (of which there are nine subdivisions): The Hinayana, or "lesser vehicle", containing the Shravaka Yana and the Pratyekabuddha Yana; the Mahayana, or "greater vehicle", which is also known as the Bodhisattva Yana; and the six Yanas of the Vajrayana—Kriya, Upa, Yoga, Mahayoga, Anu and Ati.

No one can embark upon the path without the preparation of the Hinayana, without developing the evolutionary tendencies, the readiness for the path. In this sense the teachings could be said to be secret, for, if a person is not ready for the teachings, he won't be able to hear them. Thus, they are self-secret.

The first recognition of the dharma begins with the Shravaka Yana—that is to say, listening to and hearing the teachings of the Four Noble Truths. The student hears the self-evident problems of life, the evidence for the existence of suffering, and is inspired to look further to find the origin of pain. He is inspired to search out a master who can show him the path towards seeing pain as it is, its origin, and the understanding of suffering as the path. The student might master the application of the Eight-Fold Path and so on and come to the Pratyekabuddha Yana, the second part of the Hinayana.

In the Pratyekabudda Yana one works backward, using the intellect, from death to ignorance, and so comes to the conclusion of confusion. However, there is still a tendency towards isolation in that the student is still involved with his own world, his own experience of confusion or its absence. And so it follows that the meditation practice in this yana is purely centralised on the simplicity of nowness. The student is constantly disciplining himself to stay in the now. This is true of the shamatha practice of exclusive awareness as well as of the vipassana practice of panoramic awareness.

Then, as the experience of vipassana grows, one approaches the third yana, the Bodhisattva Yana where the individual's self-conscious search is surrendered to the selflessness of the Bodhisattva ideal. Here the work lies in the acts of compassion of the Bodhisattva, compassion being the act of radiation of intense warmth, radiation without a radiator. This is, quite simply, the application of the Six Paramitas of the Bodhisattva, the action of the Nirmanakaya Buddha.

From this action one develops the transcendental knowledge of egolessness. Here the karmic chain reactions dealt with in the previous yana are absent. The two-fold veil of conflicting emotions and primitive beliefs about reality is rent—which is the same as saying that one no longer believes in the existence of an individual "I" and that the conceptualisations which this "I" laid on the real world no longer exist. This discovery—of the absence of duality and conceptualisation— is called sunyata or nothingness. Having removed the wall between *this* and *that*, the vision of *that* is clear and precise.

But, after all, the experience of shunyata, at this point, cannot be said to be nothing, because there is still some self-consciousness connected with the experience—in that the absence of duality is so vivid. So that the tenth stage of the Bodhisattva path is where one experiences the "death" of shunyata and the "birth" into luminosity. Shunyata as an experience falls away and the Bodhisattva sees, not only the absence of the barrier, but he sees further into the luminous quality of *that* which is known as the luminosity of prabhasvara of the Bodhisattva experience.

But even the notion of that experience is a hang-up, and the powerful weapon of the vajra-like samadhi is necessary to bring the Bodhisattva into the state of being wise rather than knowing wisdom as an external discovery. That is the moment of *bodhi* or *wakefulness*. Having that knowing wisdom as something external, the first discovery is that of the energies clearly seen—the mandala spectrum. Thus the experience of the vajra-like samadhi is the death of the luminosity as an external experience and the birth into the Sambhogakaya, the entrance into the Vajrayana.

Here colours speak through, as do shapes and movements, until the point is reached where there is no room for a speck of dirt. The perception of the energies for the first time is so intense and overwhelming that one is tremendously impressed by their purity. Here you regard yourself as a servant, for the very reason that you are overwhelmed by the purity of the universe. So you employ thousands of ways of communicating to the universe in terms of bodily purity, mantras and mudras.

The perception of reality as energies is tantra, and the basic notion of the tantric attitude toward the universal energies is to see them in terms of the dakini principle. That is to say, the dakinis represent the creative-destructive patterns of life. In the Kriya Yana one is overwhelmed by the brilliant purity of the energies. The falling away of this experience of purity is the entrance into the next yana, the Upa Yana.

The Upa Yana could be said to be a transitional yana in

that, in terms of application, it is dependent on both the Kriya and Yoga Yanas. Instead of seeing a pure universe, one becomes aware of the creative-destructive aspects of the energies. This is the meditation of the Yoga Yana, while one still applies the yogic practices of the Kriya. Here one begins to produce the tantric notion of intellect. This is to say that here one realises the miraculous quality of the birth of the energies, and so begins to look forward, inferring that there are more miracles to come. Such intellectuality on the vajra scale automatically brings the obstacle of a longing for a higher goal such as the "eight great miracles", and so on. But no obstacle can stand in the way here, for the tantric knowledge of the Kriya and Upa Yanas is based on the awakened state of mind of Mahamudra. Mahamudra means the Great Symbol, symbol or spectacle—vision, in terms of seeing the universe on its absolute level. This perception is so intense that all clingings and longings are only temporary. Since such a thing as this absolute could and does exist in terms of the relativity of the striving towards it, the application of these tantric methods could be described in terms of a river running towards the south—it proves that there is a mighty ocean ahead.

Next is the Yoga Yana. Here the perception of the dakini-principle is so precise that the universe is seen in terms of the three-fold mandala—the external situation, the physical body, and the state of consciousness. All these elements are equally part of *that*. In this yoga one achieves the four mudras: whatever you see is the mirror-like wisdom, whatever you hear is discriminating wisdom, whatever you feel is the wisdom of equanimity, whatever you perceive is the wisdom of automatic fulfilment. This spontaneous four-fold wisdom diffuses the boundary between centre and fringe of the mandala; thus, there is less distinctive evaluation of the mandala. Here the Mahamudra experience begins to develop toward Maha Ati. This is the entrance into the Dharmakaya.

The Way of the Buddha

Here the Mahayoga Yana begins with the union of great joy, Mahasukha. Such a breakthrough of devaluation of centre and projection brings comfort so that the vajra intellect of the Yoga Yana ceases to be a strain. This brings the joy of the union and the Ati quality of openness, so that whatever is perceived is the expression of the eight-fold primeval mandala, which need not be sought from the point of view of the Kriya Yana. Having seen that open space, as has been said, when the dawn of vajrasattva breaks, there is a complete view of the eight sacred mandalas of the eight herukas. The perception of Mandala dissolves into complete devaluation of what is. This is the entrance into Anu Yoga.

With the breakthrough of the physical nadis and chakras one begins to see the union of space and wisdom: that is, the non-substantial quality of the wisdom and the non-substantial quality of the perceiver. Even the notion of union dissolves and one begins to develop the vajra pride that you are the heruka; that acknowledging self as heruka is irrelevant. One begins to realise the two experiences of unborn and unoriginated, which leads to the next experience of Maha Ati.

The sharpness of insight and the notion of being wise are united. At this point the iconographical perception of the herukas and dakinis is self-liberated. Even the pulsating quality of the energy is diffused into what is known as the vajra chain. In other words, the notion of freedom itself has been freed so that the true perception of Dharmakaya is seen as extremely realistic, so much so that any question has been answered.

This is the end of the journey which need never have been made. This is the seamless web of what is.

71

Oxherding

THE OXHERDING PICTURES

I HAVE decided to include the ten oxherding pictures, a well-known Zen representation of the training of the mind, so basic that it could be considered fundamental to all schools of Buddhism. A deeper way of looking at it is in terms of spiritual development from Shravakayana to Maha Ati. In the Tibetan tradition there is an analogy of elephant herding but it refers largely only to the practice of *shamatha*. The symbolism does not go beyond the riding of the elephant. In the oxherding pictures the evolutionary process of taming the bull is very close to the Vajrayana view of the transmutation of energy. Particularly returning to the world as the expression of the compassion of the Nirmanakaya shows that the final realization of Zen automatically leads to the wisdom of Maha Ati.

1. The Search for the Bull

The inspiration for this first step, which is searching for the bull, is feeling that things are not wholesome, something is lacking. That feeling of loss produces pain. You are looking for whatever it is that will make the situation right. You discover that ego's attempt to create an ideal environment is unsatisfactory.

尋
牛
一

2. Discovering the Footprints

By understanding the origin you find the possibility of transcending this pain. This is the perception of the Four Noble Truths. You see that the pain results from the conflicts created by ego and discover the footprints of the bull, which are the heavy marks of ego in all play of events. You are inspired by unmistakable and logical conclusions rather than by blind faith. This corresponds to the Shravakayana and Pratyekabuddhayana paths.

二
見
跡

3. Perceiving the Bull

You are startled at perceiving the bull and then, because there is no longer any mystery, you wonder if it is really there; you perceive its insubstantial quality. You lose the notion of subjective criteria. When you begin to accept this perception of non-duality, you relax, because you no longer have to defend the existence of your ego. Then you can afford to be open and generous. You begin to see another way of dealing with your projections and that is joy in itself, the first spiritual level of the attainment of the Bodhisattva.

三 見牛

4. Catching the Bull

Seeing a glimpse of the bull, you find that generosity and discipline are not enough in dealing with your projections, because you have yet to completely transcend aggression. You have to acknowledge the precision of skilful means and the simplicity of seeing things as they are, as connected to fully developed compassion. The subjugation of aggression cannot be exercised in a dualistic framework—complete commitment into the compassionate path of the Bodhisattva is required, which is the further development of patience and energy.

5. Taming the Bull

Once caught, the taming of the bull is achieved by the precision of meditative panoramic awareness and the sharp whip of transcendental knowledge. The Bodhisattva has accomplished the transcendent acts (paramitas)—not dwelling on anything.

牧牛
三

6. Riding the Bull Home

There is no longer any question of search. The bull (mind) finally obeys the master and becomes creative activity. This is the breakthrough to the state of enlightenment—the Vajra-like Samadhi of the Eleventh Bhumi. With the unfolding of the experience of Mahamudra, the luminosity and colour of the mandala become the music which leads the bull home.

六
騎牛
歸家

7. The Bull Transcended

Even that joy and colour becomes irrelevant. The Mahamudra mandala of symbols and energies dissolves into Maha Ati through the total absence of the idea of experience. There is no more bull. The crazy wisdom has become more and more apparent and you totally abandon the ambition to manipulate.

七 忘牛存人

8. Both Bull and Self Transcended

This is the absence of both striving and non-striving. It is the naked image of the primordial Buddha principle. This entrance into the Dharmakaya is the perfection of non-watching—there is no more criteria and the understanding of Maha Ati as the last stage is completely transcended.

9. Reaching the Source

Since there is already such space and openness and the total absence of fear, the play of the wisdoms is a natural process. The source of energy which need not be sought is there; it is that you are rich rather than being enriched by something else. Because there is basic warmth as well as basic space, the Buddha activity of compassion is alive and so all communication is creative. It is the source in the sense of being an inexhaustible treasury of Buddha activity. This is, then, the Sambhogakaya.

返本還源

九

10. In the World

Nirmanakaya is the fully awakened state of being in the world. Its action is like the moon reflecting in a hundred bowls of water. The moon has no desire to reflect, but that is its nature. This state is dealing with the earth with ultimate simplicity, transcending following the example of anyone. It is the state of "total flop" or "old dog". You destroy whatever needs to be destroyed, you subdue whatever needs to be subdued, and you care for whatever needs your care.

十 入鄽垂手

昭和辛卯夏
富吉郎
畫並刻擢

93

Glossary of Terms

Bodhisattva—Bodhi means awakened state of mind, *sattva* means being or essence, in the sense of being without hesitation. The Bodhisattva is one who has committed himself to follow the path of compassion and the perfection of the six *paramitas*. The characteristic of the Bodhisattva is that his actions do not refer back to a centre or ego, he does not dwell in the absorption quality of meditation which is without clarity or inspiration.

Compassion—Karuna or *Nying-je* (in Tibetan) means noble heart. You cannot develop this until you have discovered the meditative state through *anapanasatti*. Once you are in the process of dealing with this state of being, then you cannot help radiating warmth; there is something which is open. In this case, *anapanasatti* means actually being aware of that relationship between inner and outer, this and that, which could be a primitive way of looking at *Shunyata*. But when you develop an open and carefree state of being, that is to say, non-dualistic, non-security-oriented, then the understanding of basic warmth arises. You are no longer involved with the conscious kindness of a pious and deliberate scene. You are able to give an open welcome since you have no territory of your own to preserve. The more you welcome others the freer you become. So the more you are involved with basic compassion, the more you welcome others without the host centralised notion of attempting to bring them into your scene.

Warning: Do not gulp down pious, idiot compassion; you have to use basic intelligence to see the situation clearly. You should be able to deal with the situation intuitively rather than as written about in books.

Crazy Wisdom—Personified as *Vidyadhara*, the holder of scientific knowledge. In this case, knowledge is not impersonal and abusive, but plays a compassionate role. This is

97

outrageous wisdom devoid of self and the common sense of literal thinking. Crazy wisdom is wild; in fact, it is the first attempt to express the dynamics of the tenth stage of the Bodhisattva, to step out with nakedness of mind, unconditioned, beyond conceptualisation. In this state, one acts purely on what is, with the qualities of earth, water, fire, space and stormy air.

Dakini—The feminine principle which is associated with wisdom. One finds many references made to the *Prajñaparamita* as being the mother of the Buddhas. It is pure knowledge, sharp intelligence, which can create chaos or harmony. As has been cautioned by Nagarjuna, misconceptions about *Prajñaparamita* or *Shunyata* are lethal, because the excitement of theoretical discovery is not in harmony with fundamental energy, particularly when one abuses these energies. But when the marriage of knowledge and intuitive skilful means takes place in conjunction with the perfection of the six *paramitas*, then everything is Buddha activity; the dance begins.

Deer—The symbol of peace and non-violence. Buddha gave his first teachings on the four noble truths (the teaching of *Dukha*) in a place called the Deer Park. The deer symbolises harmless and peaceful intelligence. But when one talks in terms of the wounded deer, it means that in spite of being harmless and pure, the deer has been wounded by negativities based on aggression. The innocent deer-like openness has been abused or blamed so that the basic simplicity and non-violence has been hurt by the aggressive and war-like quality of ego. The deer in Sarnath plays a very prominent part as an inspiration to us who are so involved in a very materialistic society.

Ego—There is no such thing as ego as a centralised entity. Ego is the product of various misunderstandings which cause ultimate panic. It ranges in degrees of sophistication from ape instinct to even the most advanced scientific exploration that is oriented towards proving oneself. As one becomes expert at this game of continually establishing a basic security then one instinctively tends to deceive oneself about the laws of reality. This is the basic twist: to see everything as relating to the fictitious Self.

Eh—The seed syllable for all-encompassing space, the womb which accommodates all creations, the mother principle. It is passiveness or emptiness.

Garuda—Symbolic mythical bird used in iconography. According to the story about the Garuda or celestial hawk, it nests in the wish-fulfilling tree of life, is full grown in the egg, and subdues the viciousness of the *Nagas* (symbolising the swamp-like quality of passion). Since it is mature from birth, it signifies absolute confidence.

Guru—Teacher. He continues in his search. As long as he does not go beyond his limitations he can impart spiritual knowledge to other people. A guru must be prepared to regard his students as also his teachers and then true communication and relationship continues. When true communication takes place there is a meeting of the minds beyond dualistic concepts. When a student has gone through the honeymoon affair with the individual guru, he begins to realise that the guru aspect plays a very important part in everyday life. He begins to perceive the colourful, dramatic and shocking demonstration of the guru's teaching in everything. The guru gives the student his own wisdom, but as it is received through the agency of someone else, spiritual pride is kept down.

Heruka—The masculine principle in tantric symbolism. The Heruka plays the partner in the *Dakini*'s dance. The translation of the word *tragthung* in Tibetan is blood drinker. This energy principle is called "blood drinker" because it is the energy of skilful means; that which makes the situation powerful and creative, that which drinks the blood of clinging, doubts and duality. Skilful means is the active aspect of knowledge and is spontaneous and precise in each situation.

Kagyüpa—The followers of the transmission lineage of Mahamudra. This particular school of Tibetan Buddhism is sometimes known as *Drupgyüd*, the tradition which means putting the meditative experience into practice following the example of Milarepa.

Karma—Karma is created from failing to see true ego-lessness. It results from the vicious circle of continually searching for security. This seems not to permit working with an enlightened attitude to prevent chain reactions. It is precise to the minute details and both body and mind are related to karmic cause and effect. As long as this self-defeating neurotic tendency continues, cause and effect of karma are perpetuated. There are other schools of thought which believe that the entire karmic force is predestined. There is a world karma, and also national, family and individual karma.

Knot of Eternity—Symbol of meditation or the mind of the Enlightened One. It is the never-ending discriminating awareness of wisdom. It is the state of being fully true, a continuous flow with no beginning and no end.

Mahamudra—The great symbol. It is one of the ultimate practices of meditation in which all experiences are transmuted into transcendental knowledge and skilful means. From the primordial intelligence and energy which arise there comes great luminosity so that the vividness of experience becomes the display of the mandala.

Glossary of Terms

Mandala—Structure or a group. The Tibetan word is *kgil khor* which means centre and periphery. It is the unification of many vast elements into one, through the experience of meditation. It is the process by which seeming chaos and complexities are simplified into patterns. It is usually presented in a diagram with a central figure (a personification of the Buddha principle) surrounded by other elements. The simplicity of the centre is experienced as the basic sanity of Buddha nature. Although the surrounding elements seem to be in chaos, one discovers in the evolution of the meditation that they are related to this centre as well. They are the various colours of emotions which are transmuted into the experience of a unified field.

Mantra—It is the way of transmuting energy through sound which is expressed by movement, breathing and speech. It is the quintessence of different energies expressed in sound. For instance—*HUM* is one-pointedness and penetration. It is incorrect to use mantra frivolously for some kind of excitement. It is rather a straight-forward meditation under the guidance of a master.

Materialism—The profit oriented and competitive mentality which could even be applied to "spiritual" activities. It is based on the neurotic need for security and expanding ego's territory. It is the paranoid fear of loss and greed for achievement which tends to permeate one's whole psychology. Materialism is the "sane" approach to gaining happiness. There's nothing wrong with it, but in the process of seeking happiness the original aim is lost. Instead of the simple primordial happiness one tries to grasp something tangible. At the end one is amazed to find that the search did not fulfil the original aim. Instead, shock and panic result.

Meditation—It is a way of stepping out of the neurotic and complicated state of ego. It is not worship, nor is it ritual.

Yet, ironically, meditation is the only way of spiritual practice. By transcending the questioning mind, meditation provides an enormous situation of free communication. It is a way of being simple—beyond the dualistic network. It is not a mental gymnastic practice.

Mudra—A symbol in the wider sense of gesture or action. It is the inspiring colour of phenomena. Also it is a symbol expressed with the hands to state for oneself and others the quality of different moments of meditation, such as touching the earth with the right hand as a witness to Buddha's freedom from emotional and mental frivolousness.

Paramitas—The six Paramitas or transcendental actions are attributes of Buddha activity. In perfecting them, one transcends the notion of a centralised ego.

> *Dana*—Generosity, giving without expectation, or opening, welcoming others. In other words, one does not establish the animal instinct of territory but anyone can help themselves "to me". As is said in the Bodhisattva disciplines, welcoming is the first gesture of the Bodhisattva. Without this, none of the other perfections could be put into practice.

> *Shila*—Morality or discipline. The excitement of the discovery or glimpse of the awakened state of mind should not be abused. One must not miss a moment of its inspiration. Equally, one must develop, with the help of panoramic awareness, stability and precision of insight and a knowledge of situations, so that the conduct of the Bodhisattva is dignified.

> *Kshanti*—Forbearance in the sense of seeing the situation and seeing that it is right to forbear and to develop patience. It is patience with intelligence, which is not put off by frivolous situations. It is forbearance which has

the inspiration to continue and is based on the *Dana Paramita* or the perfection of generosity. Whenever a situation is presented, one should get into it without hesitation rather than speculating in the ethical sense. It is a question of acting truly, neither for the benefit of ego, nor in terms of purifying oneself in an attempt to make an exhibition. It means allowing enough space to see the other person's point of view without the distorted filter of ego.

Virya—Whenever a person practises *virya* he finds delight in it, because it is not based on painfully going on and on and on, but it is a way of seeing the joyous element, of seeing that energy does not have to be forced but that it develops spontaneously. This happens by not regarding things as a duty in the puritanical or religious sense but doing them because one has already established the connection between the action and one's being.

Dhyana—Meditation or concentration. It means being watchful with that basic panoramic awareness that characterises all the other *Paramitas*. *Dhyana* is the means of stabilising oneself within the framework of seeing relationships, and thereby seeing that one can afford to open. This openness and keen meditative intelligence brings one to deal with the nowness of each new situation.

Prajña—Primordial intelligence is the key of the Bodhisattva's actions in dealing with practical details of earth and space. He develops such a sharp and penetrating sense that he can cut through the conceptualised notion of duality and see the simplicity. *Prajña* is that quality which culminates in acting spontaneously with the help of the other *Paramitas* with such precision that the spinal cord of duality is cut.

Mudra

Passion—Passion is contagious in that once you ignore the source of passion it will destroy or burn you, but once you realise that passion is another means of communicating, then it becomes basically an important way of relating yourself to mother earth or the all-encompassing womb. Passion is all-embracing in that it can transmute, as Buddha said, into discriminating awareness wisdom (*jñana*).

Reincarnation—May be more precisely termed rebirth because the accumulation of feelings, perceptions, impulses and consciousness which are the constituents of so-called spirit, do not live through as one solid thing, but are constantly changing. This state of consciousness does not belong exclusively to human beings and is not determined by the physical body. Rebirth into different lives is possible. It is a natural karmic force.

Siddhas—Great yogis who have achieved the experience of *Mahamudra* (see Crazy Wisdom entry).

Skilful Means—It is not based purely on ego-inclined common sense. If one relates to open space, then his way of perceiving the display of apparent phenomena is colourful and inspiring, so that he doesn't hesitate to deal with the situation. He simply sees the open situation, the way of unconditioned appropriate response to the nowness. Skilful means is 'the active masculine principle on the feminine ground of *prajña*.

Thought—is the production of the neurotic ego. However, sometimes it manifests as sparks of intelligence. It often shows as the playback of memories and emotions. It is largely either discursive or in pictorial form. Thoughts only possess power if one is fascinated by them. Consciousness is a tendency of dualistic projection which makes for the discrimination between subject and object. The subconscious is the underlying gossip.

Glossary of Terms

Truth—That which transcends questioning. If the truth is not absolute it is a lie.

Vajra—The symbol of indestructibility. It is also referred to as penetrating wisdom which cuts through solidified ignorance. The Tibetan equivalent *dorje* is "noble stone"; it can destroy that which seemingly cannot be destroyed.

Vam—The seed syllable of the indestructible *vajra* nature, also representing great joy. It is the principle of son or youthful prince, the active force of clear light.

Other books by CHÖGYAM TRUNGPA:

Born in Tibet
Cutting Through Spiritual Materialism
First Thought Best Thought: 108 Poems
Glimpses of Abhidharma
Journey without Goal: The Tantric Wisdom of the Buddha
Meditation in Action
The Myth of Freedom and the Way of Meditation
Shambhala: The Sacred Path of the Warrior
The Tibetan Book of the Dead (with Francesca Fremantle)

Printed in the United States
by Baker & Taylor Publisher Services